T0368422

This is My Letter to You

JOULD DANIEL

To order additional copies of this book, contact:
Xlibris
844-714-8691
www.Xlibris.com
Orders@Xlibris.com

ISBN: Softcover   979-8-3694-2898-6
         EBook   979-8-3694-2908-2

Print information available on the last page

Rev. date: 08/28/2024

Judy Ann started kindergarten in a new country after leaving her precious grandmother on the small island she was once familiar.

Her grandmother's familiar surroundings allowed Judy Ann to feel safe and comfortable. Her grandmother's yard was an adventurous place as it was expansive as half of the entire street the house sat on.

Lush trees made hiding spaces for Island kids as they played familiar games of hide and seek. On most quiet days Judy Ann would sit on the veranda and admire the sunny warm days and the aesthetics which nature provided as a backdrop of blue mountains. She never imagined leaving a place as wonderful as this.

Judy Ann's mother, who was now living in the States, longed for her and her sister and sent for them to come to America. This news brought along a mix of emotions for Judy Ann, who was excited yet somewhat saddened.

Departure day arrived and Judy Ann left behind the things that she felt would make her stand out in a new country. Things such as, her baby bottle which she drank out of for quite some time. The move held many questions for Judy Ann. She wondered what the children were like in the States. After all, she was now five years old and too big for a baby bottle.

Judy Ann left behind her stuffed teddy bear which gave her comfort at night while listening to the thunder, rain, and on dry nights crickets that blared as loud as sirens in the big cities. After all, the kids in the States might tease her for such an attachment.

Judy Ann left behind the veranda which she loved to play on and make believe the rest of the world was just as beautiful as the lush foliage from her grandmother's yard.

Judy Ann left behind the crazy stories her grandmother would tell her on the big auburn couch, on nights when it seemed there was no one else in the world but the two of them.

Judy Ann left behind the drive into town with the family in the noisy but calming blue car which will forever remind her of the island she cherished so dearly.

Judy Ann left behind the Saturday trips to the beach with the winding roads that led to an azure paradise. But most of all, Judy Ann left behind her Grandmother.

While in America Judy Ann longed to be with her grandmother on that small island once again. The first day of school spelled discomfort because Judy Ann had a strong Caribbean accent.

Judy Ann would spend a lot of time trying to pick up the American accent and eventually became acclimated to her new home. At school Judy Ann became best friends with a girl named Anna Margarita, who was just as friendly. The two were inseparable.

As the years passed, Judy Ann learned to accept her new country as her own. Even though Judy Ann longed to see her grandmother, she eventually learned to cherish the time they had together on the island. She knew that she would return to the island for the love and the memories she once left behind.

Printed in the United States
by Baker & Taylor Publisher Services